KATHLEEN PARTRIDGE'S
Tranquil Moments

To

Jessie

From

Enid with love xx

Jarrold Publishing, Norwich

GOOD WISHES
THROUGH THE YEAR

I wish for you good health in Spring,
When breezes from the sea are blowing
And time and tide on life's high seas
Bring in your dream ships gaily glowing.

I wish for you a summer garden
Softly sheltered, gay with flowers
A view from every window
To enhance the passing hours.

Happiness in Autumn
When the leaves are bronze and yellow
With matching memories
As calm and quiet, cool and mellow.

And in the Winter, may you have
Contentment and a cosy fire
But most of all companionship
Most suited to your heart's desire.

A spectacular view over Killiney Bay
from Dalkey, County Dublin

SPRING

In Spring, the loveliest of sights
Anemones and aconites,
Down woodland ways, the first sweet flowers
To tell the beauty of the hours.

And when the aconite is over
There will be crocus in the clover
Mauve and yellow, green and gold
Beneath the trees grown wise and old.

No car could travel down those lanes
Where Spring begins and Winter wanes
This is the path by footsteps trod
The haven of a gracious God.

So sings the heart this golden morn
The first song that was ever born
For fragrant air and spring delights
Anemones and aconites.

Crocus buds bloom in the
spring sunshine

A quaint thatched cottage near Canterbury, Kent

WOOED BY THE SPRING

Leaves that are bursting open
Daffodil buds uncurled
This is the giving of glory
The offer of gold to the world.

Wherever a garden is tended
Wherever a meadow is blessed
There will be daffodils dancing
By the kiss of the Spring caressed.

Few can resist the charm of a cluster of daffodils

BLESS YOU

God be with you in the morning
In the sunshine or the rain
In the magic of each moment
As the day begins again.

God be with you in the evening
When the day has reached its goal
When all creatures cuddle closely
And the lamb bleats near the foal.

Though life's duties are demanding
And your path is not sublime
Through the ups and downs of living
God be with you friend of mine.

Mare and foal graze near Sharpitor, Devon

Shepherd with friends, Dumfries and Galloway

Delightful spring scene at Stanway, Gloucestershire

WHEN GOD SMILES

Stamen by stamen and leaf by leaf
The earth grows lovely beyond belief
Blade after blade the grass renews
The lush green colour of wayside views.

Primrose by primrose the air grows sweet
Mixing and making the Spring complete
Sunbeam by sunbeam for miles and miles
The world grows fairer because God smiles.

Primroses brighten even a dull March day

STEPPING-STONES

In the music of the morning
Where the shadows meet and blend
The water chases sunbeams
As it hurries to descend.

And so the world makes merry
With the green and golden tones
And the fretful fuss of living
Grows as smooth as stepping-stones.

The Tarr Steps –
an unusual crossing point on the
River Barle, Exmoor

BLUEBELL TIME

Let me laze and let me linger
Though the world be in a hurry
Until I find the bluebells
In the sunny woods of Surrey.

They never fail or falter
Come what may in any year
I will waken one fine morning
And the bluebells will be here.

I scarce believe in Springtime
Till I gaze upon that view
Of so many little flowers
Massed to make the earth so blue.

A colourful carpet of bluebells in Sheringham Park, Norfolk

Spring arrives with a flourish in Dartmoor

These tulips create a riot of colour near Spalding,
Lincolnshire

WHERE TULIPS GROW

To see a mass of tulips red
In any field or garden bed
Proud and upright, cool and clean
Folded round in wraps of green

Makes me see the world anew
In tones as loyal and as true
Where men uphold a friend and neighbour
And rest contented after labour.

The graceful tulip is always a favourite

FLEDGLING

He bursts his shell in Spring
And sets his song to nature's lilt
His eyes will open to the view
Of blossoms over-split.

From ivy leaf to courtyard wall
From chimney-pot to glen
He'll know the haunts of squirrels
As he knows the homes of men.

He'll see as much of Heaven
As he sees of mother earth
These wonders are his heritage
Right from his hour of birth.

Young bullfinches prepare to leave the nest

A garden warbler feeds her offspring

SUMMER

If one sweet summer day
Can blend the sound and scent together
To be remembered always
As the ideal summer weather.

If just one rose is perfect
Be it yellow, be it white
Then shall it make a memory
To carry through the night.

And we shall lift our eyes
To find serenity anew
In the heavenly mingling
Of the silver with the blue.

And all the goodness of the earth
Shall shine in glad array
As if a lifetime's loveliness
Lived in one summer's day.

Summertime in East Hagbourne,
Oxfordshire

WAKE UP AND SING

High hills bring hopeful thoughts
And happy hearts make helpful deeds
Now is the time to gather flowers
Where friendship plants the seeds.

The time for looking up old friends
And going on the spree
For a trip along the river
Or an outing to the sea.

Peace and quiet on Loch Morlich, near Aviemore

Negotiating the locks on the Caldon Canal in Staffordshire

Looking down on delightful Cawsand Bay in Cornwall

HOLIDAY TIME

Leave the world of commerce
And let nature call the tune
Idling in a haze
Of golden sand and tufted dune.

Brook no interruptions
In the sweet untroubled hours
And taste the morning fragrance
In the scent of many flowers.

And when the sky and ocean
Meet and blend in heavenly blue
Then will the heart refreshed
Be as contented as the view.

Instow in Devon – far from the madding crowd

HOME TO FRIENDS

Laughter is like summer sunshine
When the day is born
The heart's content is in the gold
That glorifies the dawn.

So when refreshing showers fall
And bathe the world with dew
Then let me sing the day away
And let me laugh with you.

This typically English thatched cottage is in
Corfe Castle, Dorset

Time ticks slowly by in Burford, Cotswolds

East Hendred in Oxfordshire is a haven of old world charm

TIME AND TIDE

Time and the flowing streams of life
Make changes on the earth around
Villages emerge as towns
That were by old-world customs bound.

Trees spread or fall and rivers widen
Brooks run dry and forests grow
We always find some changes
In the views we used to know.

Gomshall Mill in Surrey is a popular place to stop
for a while

BANK HOLIDAY

Blue water for serenity
White sails when hope runs high
No finer sight to lift the heart
Than sails against the sky.

So make this day a holiday
From all the usual things
Listen to the carefree songs
A bird in Summer sings.

Let no troubles cloud your view
No wilful words annoy
Just sing a song for happiness
And say a prayer for joy.

Time off at Barton Broad, Norfolk

A perfect day for a sail on the Norfolk Broads

Green fields and forest stretch to the horizon from
Scotts View, Borders

MEASURE FOR MEASURE

The earth is the Lord's, I am His guest
His couch it is on which I rest.
His flock of birds sweet music trill
Upon my sunny windowsill.

His fields and hills my solace are
The morning dew, the evening star
The fullness of the land and sea
These precious gifts He trusts with me.

Seagulls hover above Ullapool, Highlands

THE PRICE OF FISH

There is a tale of the ships and the sea
Of stormy weather and bravery
Of lifeboat launching as waves grow steeper
And the lonely life of a lighthouse keeper.

But the sea takes its toll and the men grow old
And the bravest stories are seldom told
And what do we know of the havoc wrought?
Of the hazards life when the fish are caught?

A traditional fishing boat at Hastings, Sussex

Godrevy lighthouse stands watch from Godrevy Island,
Cornwall

This tranquil landscape can be admired from Alderley Edge,
Cheshire

SERENITY

The flowers talk, yet do not need an answer.
The grasses sigh, and yet they are not sad.
The leaves are rustling one against the other
To tell of all the lovely days we've had.

There's so much movement that is never restless
And so much sound that does not interrupt,
The winds are whistling wisdom in the hedges
In tones that are not tiring nor abrupt.

And that is why the earth contains such solace
Harmonious to hear and cool to touch.
For nature has so many lovely voices,
And yet she never seems to talk too much.

The exquisite gardens at Leonardslee, Sussex

AUTUMN

Mellow weather, tweeds and heather
Golden grows the gorse.
Beech leaves turning, creeper burning
Grass becoming coarse.

Fields of stubble, brooks that bubble
Lanes with rainbow ruts.
Hedges looped with blackberries
And bushes decked with nuts.

Hips and haws by scores and scores
And honey from the bees.
Mushrooms in the dewy dell
And moss beneath trees.

A world of wealth and wonder
Where the leaves dance as they fall
And all we lack is just the time
To go and see it all.

Leaves start to turn in
Sherwood Forest, Nottinghamshire

Swaledale, North Yorkshire seems untouched
by the march of time

THE SCENT OF AUTUMN

Autumn is scented with fruit that has fallen
The burning of bonfires and turning of loam
Mists in the morning, so faintly refreshing
And smoke from the chimneys that beckon me home.

Late flowering roses distil their sweet perfume
Blending along with the thyme and the mint
But the smell of nasturtiums, this flower of the Autumn
Is rioting colour that blooms without stint.

Autumn berries brighten the guelder rose

OUR TREE

May life for you be like this gracious tree
Rooted in strength and grown in majesty
Defying storms, although it still achieves
To catch the sunlight filtering through the leaves.

This stately tree, as quiet as a psalm
Where birds may nestle in her knotted arm
And rest in safety, rocking as they trill
Surveying spire and mansion, vale and hill.

A shelter for the ones who come and go
At peace with God, good friends with those below
Maturing wisely through each growing stage
Upright in youth and beautiful in age.

Sunset over Hickling Broad, Norfolk

Golden leaves cover the ground at Burnham Beeches, Buckinghamshire

Unloved by farmers, the poppy nevertheless brightens the English countryside

HARVEST

Some of the seeds we planted
May not flourish it is true
But life still has a harvest
For the aims that we pursue.

In nature as in life
We plan our way and sow our seeds
And in God's time and season
Reap the harvest of our deeds.

Harvest time at Iona Abbey, Strathclyde

GROWING OLD

It is the Autumn of the year
That makes the harvest moon appear
To shine upon the glowing gold
Of lovely leaves now growing old.

And may the self-same beauty grace
The contours of a gentle face
That time has touched and left still fair
And shining with the kindness there.

Seasons change at Clumber Park in Nottinghamshire

Glencayne Woods, Ullswater is the perfect spot for an
autumn stroll

Denver Mill, Norfolk – a reminder of days gone by

AUTUMN SUNSHINE

A shower of autumn sunbeams
Golden flecks among the brown
Mild days and mellow moments
Fashion earth a golden gown.

Capture it and keep it
For a memory in your mind
Look at it and love it
Ere the year leaves it behind.

And one day you will remember
How your eyes became awake
To a shower of autumn sunbeams
That were falling in a lake.

Derwent Reservoir nestles in the Derbyshire Peak District

A FRESH START

May God wipe out our failures
As the night blacks out the day
And while we sleep fold up our cares
And send our fears away.

Thus every day we start afresh
Upon a spotless page
This is the morning gift of God
Our earthly heritage.

Tawstock Church in North Devon provides the final touch
to this idyllic setting

Time to reflect at Loch Broom, Highlands

Tumbling waters of the Afon Dyfi at Dinas Mawddwy, Merioneth

RISE AND FALL

I want no rushing torrents
Just a peaceful drifting stream
And a jagged piece of rock
So shaped that I may sit and dream.

With tranquil falling foliage
Beside the water's brink
And leaves that sail the ripples
Dancing once, before they sink.

The beauty spot of Epping Forest, a world away
from nearby London

WINTER

The garden sleeps and dreams
Now that the season's work is ended
A sense of peace and idleness
Has all the world befriended.

The hardy blossoms that are left
Look tattered and forlorn
Only the berries shine for joy
And wait for Christmas morn.

And so there is serenity
About the garden dreaming
Duty is fulfilled
There is no reason now for scheming.

The last tired leaf relaxing
Finds it only has to fall
And earth waits in her wisdom
With a resting place for all.

A blanket of snow transforms this
everyday scene near Whaley Bridge,
Derbyshire.

WINTER WAYS

Winter ways are wonderful
When happy hearts make fun
Beside the icy waters
That are glistening in the sun.

A fairyland of wisdom
In the filigree of frost
Where the golden leaves have fallen
And the foliage is lost.

There is merriment and music
Found in woodland paths that freeze
From a rainbow in a puddle
Or a star caught in the trees.

The River Ure flows through wintry Wensleydale,
North Yorkshire

A silver birch stands frozen in time

A solitary figure trudges through the snow near
Canterbury, Kent

HOUSE WARMING

Cold are the mornings and dark the night
But the glowing fires are a welcome sight
Though branches sigh when the east wind blows
A Christmas tree in the window glows.

And Winter must change one day to Spring
Trees must blossom and birds must sing
And clouds turn silver that looked so black
And all life's sunbeams be welcomed back.

Frost can lend nature a touch of pure magic

LIFE IS A PRAYER

What fitter prayer could be designed
Than little actions that are kind!
Is there a better living creed
Than sympathy in time of need?

What greater psalm of hymn of praise
That cheerfulness and courteous ways
For who can love the Lord God when
He loves not first his fellow-men?

The choir of Norwich Cathedral in full voice

Norwich Cathedral on a still winter's day

In winter, aconites and snowdrops add a welcome
splash of colour

WINTER FLOWERS

Where paths are frosty, woods are wet
I haven't seen a snowdrop yet
But am enjoying the sensation
Of living in anticipation.

One day when the snow is shrinking
And I am glancing down unthinking
There will be snowdrops, white and sweet
Encased in green about my feet.

And if by chance the time is right
To find a winter aconite
Then will I say with words sincere
'O what a happy time of year.'

These aconites struggle to bloom on the coldest winter's day

BECAUSE OF YOU

Can you say at close of day
Before you meet the night
Of all the troubles in the world
You helped to put one right?

That just one heart was happier
Because your smile was true
One wrinkle in the folds of life
Was smoothed . . . because of you.

A layer of snow completes the picture in unspoilt Norfolk

ISBN 0-7117-0346-9 © Copyright Jarrold Publishing 1988. Reprinted 1989, 1992. Designed and produced by Parke Sutton Limited for Jarrold Publishing, Norwich. Printed in Portugal.